Hope Wears a Cowboy Hat

Hope Wears a Cowboy Hat

Poems by

Mary M. Sesso

Cover art by Jerilyn Sodee
Author photo by Lisa M. Sodee

ISBN: 978-1-63980-764-2

Kelsay Books
502 South 1040 East, A-119
American Fork, Utah 84003
Kelsaybooks.com

*for my family with love
and in memory of Eric*

Acknowledgments

Many thanks to my workshop friends who helped craft these poems and a special thanks to the editors of the following journals in which these poems appeared:

Burgeon Magazine: "Driving Behind *Zill's Body Parts* Truck,"
  "Mom's Morning Ritual," "*Quando Bella*"
Cardinal Sins: "Flowers Unfasten the Cold"
Cutbank Literary Journal: "Soon"
Emerge Literary Journal: "Prayer," "Praise the Unexpected"
Her Word: "One Woman's Guide to Happiness"
Loch Raven Review: "Orange and Black," "Time," "Touch Scars,"
  "Turning Point," "Why I Love Emily Dickinson"
Medical Literary Messenger: "Summer Is Ending"
Mid Atlantic Review: "Hope Wears a Cowboy Hat," "Popsicle
  Dream," "Waiting for a Hospital Bed"
One Art: "White Gloves"
The Ravens Perch: "Burning Leaves," "Light and Shade,"
  "Writer's Prompt"

Contents

You only live once,
but if you do it right,
once is enough.

—May West

Praise the Unexpected

after Martin Espada

Praise the drop of blood
growing on my shirt that holds
a surprise, and for the first time,
watching a flock of chickadees
mob a red-shouldered hawk,
sullying the air with noise.

Praise stars that go to bed with you,
the rosebush, naked for months,
dressing in red after a whisper of rain,
and nightmares surrendering
to the pillow saying *If you don't
like us, write your own.*

Praise nights that let daylight
sleepwalk through darkness, a rainbow
pinched awake when rain dries its hands,
and a red moon eclipsing the sun,
so cocky it thinks it can burn down
the sky.

Fluttering

You keep on trying not to speak
of death, or how you're the owner
of a heart that's been startled by
atrial flutter.

Flutters aren't pretty like butterfly wings—
They might let blood clots ascend
to the brain, clipping your wings
and leaving you speechless.

That's why you work to remember good times,
like eating plump raspberries on your cereal
before going to school, how you were tempted
to steal Butterfingers but didn't.

Memories have been flying off gray matter
for years. You aren't sure if the moon
really looked you in the eye every night
when you were little before you pulled down

the shade making you feel safe. Or did
you ever feel love hot as a dandelion
in the sun? Your heart says yes and wants
to be believed.

Driving Behind *Zill's Body Parts* Truck

We don't throw away hearts in trouble.
We open them, drop in stents
and valves to restore health,
crumbly knees mate with fake ones
and suddenly smile.

But I worry about my spirit.
Is there a replacement for a cranky
one, so full of crank
it can't renew itself to keep from
going off the tracks?

I hold a mirror, peer inside.
It's like swallowing a camera.
I see a soul desperate to pink up its cheeks,
a ventricle cracked with murky longings,
hope stumbling over its feet.

If my spirit had a sponsor, she would say,
Turn away from an image of a woman
too grizzled to dance. Like Zill,
you're able to replace broken parts
with ones that work.

My Father at Seventy-Three

His hair is wavy white, skin lines run deep until
they run out and bones speak softly. His heart
cries out loud when it makes

a fist louder than his voice. Nitroglycerine sings
a lullaby, keeps soothing until it doesn't,
and fingered rosary beads speak silently.

All his life he hunted and fished. Once while
wading, casting his rod, he whistled past
a mother bear behind a bush to let her know
he was moving on.

When his heart is quiet, he soft-shoes it
in the sand on a Lake Michigan beach to feed
Canada geese that refuse

to migrate. He carries a bag of corn on his
shoulder and when the geese see him, he's a star,
his admirers honking, rushing the stage

while he raises his hand to broadcast the food,
like Fred Astaire tapping, throwing aloft his cane,
each man creating his own special dance.

Mom's Morning Ritual

As soon as the sun's up, she works
to tame the knotty blue snakes
that crawl up her legs, dragging pain,
past the hips and into the vaginal wall.
She encloses them, ankle to groin,
inside miles of ace bandages,
releasing them at bedtime. The strength
of their bite, so strong, so stinging,
sometimes wakes the night,
rupturing a vein black and blue.

Under the moon, deer dance on air legs
in nearby woods. What a shame
Mom can't step under that aura.
Pain would refuse to come, night would sleep
and gravity wouldn't be crouching,
ready to wake the snakes.

Popsicle Dream

*. . . but behind all your stories is
always your mother's story,
because hers is where yours begins.*
—Mitch Albom

Novenas to Our Mother of Perpetual Help
work to stare down the shadow
that follows her as she carries mop
and bucket up and down stairs,
into the kitchen where bushels of peaches,
plums, pears wait to be canned for children
whose stomachs are filled with hunger.
In this world, love keeps itself in the dark,
though the trace of a caress on the shoulder
stirs the air if highballs don't rough it up.

Does she ever have a popsicle dream
where maid turns into princess? With
parted lips and half-shut eyes, she dances
under the moon until the sky torches itself.
Gaudy. Red, like the skirt she swirls.

Summer Is Ending

My patient's face is as barren after surgery
as a storm-damaged oak when limbs fall off.
The loss of bone and flesh highlight eyes
that shine blue fierceness.

His words ink on a pad—he has no voice.
A gentle man, he asks me for a towel
to hold close to his neck in case cancer
bursts through an artery causing an explosion
of fatal red.

His doctor had offered a choice. Surgery
to remove the mass, or to sit on your porch in Texas
and rock away the rest of your time and be
comfortable. Pain pills can be your buddy.
Surgical cures are iffy and summer will soon
be ending, he said.

Waiting for My Hospital Bed

Time waits where flowers bloom
on walls and a cardinal sits on a branch
with leaves reddening but never falling.
I wonder about silver trees through
the window until I grow silver myself.
The one comfort: any illness hiding
in my body like a trapped animal
will soon be set free.

The late hour bites its lip and anxiety
chaps them. Nurses say *Soon* though
I know it's a sweet white lie.
Before the peach fuzz of dawn rises,
I want to fall into a bed as gently as
a pillow feather falling through air.

Touch Scars

When I was a girl, my mother placed
a silver Miraculous Medal around my neck,
believed the Virgin Mother would keep me safe.
And no one in a slouched hat followed me
home after school dances and no eager boy
tried to sneak me into the utility room.
But unsafe men were everywhere in plain sight,
like the painter who patted my rump more
than once, the optometrist who pinched
my nipple, the priest who lifted my plaid skirt
after daily Mass.

The worst was the neighbor whose kids
I was baby-sitting when I was thirteen.
His big sweaty body bullied me into a corner,
grabbing, trying to lift my sweater,
his thick legs trying to pin me against the wall,
until I was able to twist away and run home.

Each time I told my mother what happened
and each time *she* whispered:
Don't tell your father. He'll kill him.
I think she feared a bullet from the snub nose
he kept under his pillow would shoot blame
directly at me.

To keep my daughters safe, I give them
words to hold close: *No! Stop!*
Scream if you must. And remember,
badness doesn't just crawl through a window,
hide under a bed or in a closet. Badness
can be like a seed burst from a plant, right
in front of your eyes.

Small Town

Some secrets go to the grave, some get itchy,
scratch the tongue to become words,
like whose husband's car was spotted
during the night at another woman's house.

Other secrets can't help shouting out loud
like a black eye trying to hide under
a feathered hat at Sunday Mass, and a boy
coming into the world who looks like a father,
just not the one married to his mother

There are ones that are whispered:
the dentist who pinches the nipples of girls while
they're imprisoned in his chair, and the teen-
age girl who disappears for a few months,
visiting an aunt and comes back thinner.

Sunlight forces its way through windows
washing away shadows while secrets sneak out.
When they leave the room, they write their
own poem.

Quando Bella

Zia's leg bones and spine
curve into rickets. Her mother's
life had ended when hers began
seventy years ago. A teat
at the end of a cloth bag, filled
with anything wet, nursed her into life.
Like a bud cheated of sun,
the hope of becoming slipped away.

Sadness now breaks morning.
Her sister died last week leaving
her heart tangled in grief and loosening
tears against my shoulder.
When it's time to leave, her smile
droops, chin quivers.
To cheer her up, I say, "Sing to me,
Zia, of the soldier boy in Napoli
and music playing by the sea."
Sitting on a low stool, keeping time
with her cane and in a clear contralto,
she sings,
Si, si, mi amerai,
quando bella me vidrai . . .

(You will fall in love with me
when you see how beautiful I am.)

Boiling Down Tree Sap to Make Maple Syrup

Sometimes the highest chair in the house
is a rickety highchair, and Mother can't resist
its siren song to climb and wash,
move baby doll Betsy Westy off the tray, then
ready a pail of water and soapy sponge—

She climbs up, stands on the seat and turns
slowly, like a music box doll, raising her arm
to start scrubbing. Sometimes fate sharpens
its knife and a chair leg can't remember to stand up
straight. It shatters, like Mother's knee when
she falls. Now her agility lives in the past tense
and time holds pain close to its chest like a toy puppy.
And the scent of maple sweetness seizes the air.

Flowers Unfasten the Cold

I remember my husband, how he loved
his Queen Elizabeth roses.
One November two blooms hung on
even though winter was bragging
how dark it was. I touched the petals.
It's as if I were standing on the rim
of that darkness and their softness
kept me from falling in.

By March I will remember why
darkness will step back:
because spring steps forward and sun
fills the eyes with sky, flowers unfasten
the cold and the color green sounds
like a calliope, because I know
kissing fire may kill me with smoke,
but especially because love
is for keeps even when memory
forgets how to lean on itself.
If love and sadness were flowers,
they'd be in the same bouquet.

Tell Me Again

Joe prepares for cancer's finale by eating tiny meals
and telling me again how to survive a universe

of wills, bills, bank accounts, and taxes.
It's not easy like fixing the roof, stumping trees

this business of how to end one's life. He no longer
wants to smoke, though cigarillo funk wanders in

and out of rooms and sleeps on the sofa. A speck
of his pasta hides on a chair back.

Last month he'd draped the strands on it to dry,
handling them as if they were pearls.

He thinks I'm not listening, and like a shot
from a cap gun shouts, *I'll spit on your grave.*

These words don't hurt, but my heart wakes up to his desire
that I manage after he's gone. *Tell me again,* I say.

I need to get this right.

Burning Leaves

When summer walks to the edge,
it doesn't take long for the maples
to arrange the sky with leaf flames.
I don't think of death when it's time
for them to die and fall to the ground.
And I don't need to see you again
to remember how you hauled leaves
to the street in your wooden wheelbarrow
and burned them at the curb while
singing *La donna e mobile.*

Though my memory consorts with thieves,
this image is safe, even when the sun
is late and the moon refuses to shine.

Hope Wears a Cowboy Hat

I don't think of all the misery,
but the beauty that remains.
—Anne Frank

My son's face is all axes and knives
because he finds out he has cancer,
not from the doctor, but by the tech asking
if he wants to take part in a chemo study.
He feels like a bullet is aimed at his heart
that only hope can stop.

Hope is hard to hang onto. It's like trying to
remember last night's dream or stop
a hundred buckets of honey from emptying
all at the same time. My spirit says wait,
give it time to grow muscle, but waiting
is tough on the body. Stomach acid
has no shut-off valve, skin wets itself
and dreams stick a finger in your eye.

Before the moon finds reasons to lose
its shine, I make peace in my tug-of-war
with hope. It's time for Eric to put on
his second-hand, stringy cowboy hat
and play some cool jazz.

A Scrim of Snow

for Eric

A late March wind lashes a lady slipper
in the woods at the end of the street.
The flower's giving-pink comforts
a tired winter. I want to remember
this lovely image though it will fade
as more winters pass.

You've begun to fade, too. I try to remember
your laughter, but it's as if the sun can't find
its way to spring and you're lost in a scrim
of snow. Though your face is disappearing,
I won't stop trying to find it, even if summer
comes and blooms just for me.

Turning Point

I'm tired of losing friends. Three were close.
They came into my life the last time I figured
we were young. We listened to Herb Alpert—
A Taste of Honey, Whipped Cream, The Lonely Bull,
and shared stories about kids, complaints
about husbands, how tough the balance could be.

There are ways to stop growing old. Darlene's
angry pistol finally got it right, though her depression
hid behind *haute couture.* Jean tried to die how many
times before hijacked pills reached critical mass.
She was found by her daughter, who in college,
died the same way. Then there's Martha
whose body lost its fierceness. Its flesh let the spirit
flicker away because lymphoma told it to.

This minute I'm sitting pretty listening to music,
not thinking about loss, but I feel like my house
was on fire, and I was lucky to have made it out alive.

Eclipse

On earth it's easy to study
how stars hold up the sky
and how a chubby moon
washes out meteors,
but hard to surrender
to a mirror where once
you dreamed a pretty girl,
how you bent light, and life
left fingerprints the colors
of hair bows.

My reflection says old age
is too tired to catch night's
luster. I've become an eclipse
and must make peace with
a morning sky supersized
with fire.

Writing Prompt

I Imagine I'm alone on the 14th floor
in an empty building.
The carpeting is red. I feel like
I'm inside a crimson oyster shell,
a darkroom of loneliness with
nothing to break the quiet.

Scarlet reaches out with stinky hands
like the mean boy who grabbed me
after school, the one who laughed
and called me a pirate
when I walked into the classroom
with glasses and one eye patched.

Since I'm not locked in this building,
how do I walk out of my head
and forgive red thoughts, rub it's
stain off my imagination? Maybe
tonight, despite weak eyes, I'll paint
dreams in pastels.

Time

When spider webs unite, they can tie up a tiger
—Ethiopian saying

The start of a spider web caught
my eye yesterday when I saw
a single strand stretching from
its y-shaped anchor on the rib of
the patio umbrella all the way
to the chair. This morning
there is a blanket of silk.
With a little time, I might discover
how the clever sun spills silver
on the threads and how something
finer than a baby's eyelash
hosts a bite that kills. With even
more time, I could learn how
to play these delicate strings.

White Gloves

Yesterday a katydid was keeping me company
on the patio when a praying mantis snatched it.
That must be why my dreams are scary—
I'm afraid the clock might run out while I'm enjoying
the sun, and suddenly it's dark black with no
leftover green bits of summer.

Time, like a butler in white gloves doesn't care
if I'm katydid gentle or if my bite doesn't hurt.
Last night I dreamed he brushed sand
off his fingers, and suddenly I was filled with a fear
of the dark. Then I watched him exit with a murmur
of sun in his eye.

Everywhere

Because it's February, Spring turns her eye north,
says she's stealing the south's thunder,
striking up the band early so snowdrops can
surprise the cold with a kiss.

Because it's February, the maple doesn't scold
its limbs for failing to pull on a green dress,
but frowns for wearing flowers two weeks
before expected.

Because it's February, rivers are full
of themselves, mud slides have their way
with houses, and the sea, acting like a mad lover,
can't help grabbing the land hugging it.

In the north, February acts all innocent,
does its best to hide warnings of danger
among forsythia and cherry blossoms,
hoping we can't see signs of change.

Orange and Black

Enough of snowflakes and cold.
The deep snow's hands are heavy,
icy gray, and hold down
my forsythia as if kneeling

on a hard pew to pray, and covering up
two early yellow blossoms. If I could
carry a tune, I'd sing gray a requiem
while I pray for tulip and dogwood

blooms; or wait for the Baltimore oriole
to sing, a lyric tenor all gussied up
in black and orange, colors so wild
you'd think sunset and night stole

each other's drama. Enough of cold and ice.
It makes the air so quiet I can hear it.

Light and Shade

A healthy maple outside my condominium
is being cut down. Perhaps it's not
the sharp wind rattling its arms,
but outrage at the chain saw killer,
screeching at 120 decibels. If the tree
had legs, it would run away.

Who can say the maple doesn't feel pain
as limbs are sliced off and stump ground
into sawdust? I think about its cousins
in the woods that eat nails to give us
maple syrup until they can't sugar anymore,
then the saw.

How do I mourn this giant neighbor
yet open my eyes to the grave-flowers
of bright yellow petunias, like sundrops,
ready to be planted on top of its remains?

One Woman's Guide to Happiness

Her shadow keeps dancing when she sits.
Tired sex fades into a pear blossom in a vase.
Death backs out the door, waves goodbye and blows a kiss.
Dust picks itself up, jumps out the window and plays with dirt.
A banjo in the hall closet strums zydeco if the blues over-stay.
The gun in her depressed husband's pocket refuses to fire.
Her roar is a wild tiger lily held in a fist.
The sun plays dress-up in the multi-striped curtains.
When a book flips open, verbs turn smart-alecky.
A zebra mocha is her drug of choice.

Wants and Wishes

for Allison May

My granddaughter's watermelon belly,
is ripe with girl promise.
I wish her to be born with a mouth
that blows spit bubbles when she chews
her toes, but also tastes the sweet milk
of wisdom; lets truth caress her tongue
like syrup on pancakes and not distrust it
like she will with the first spoonful of peas.

If sleep is troubled, I want her to laugh
when the sun is stuck to the sky or when clouds
roughshod under it. I want her to dream ideas
bright as a river rippling with stars. Most of all,
I want her see the world with the clearness
of a cloudless moon and when the sky spreads
its dazzle-blue, almost touching her hand
without even asking.

Soon

for Poppy

I never knew I loved the sun
until it curled up on the living room
rug and invited the old dog to nap
in its warmth. I shake the past
out of my pocket and look for the list
new things to love, like a great grandchild
soon to be born. I won't mind if she cries.
She'll lean against my shoulder,
feel my warm hands cupping her head
that tell her she's safe, how she'll learn
to love many things, like dandelions,
how they'll never shut the door on yellow,
but scatter it to get her attention,
and the blue sky.

Why I Love Emily Dickinson

Tell all the truth but tell it slant
—Emily Dickinson

I love slant truth. It's like living
in a world of play where clarity
takes a back seat. When I told
my friend her painting was full
of colorful moods, I really meant
it looked sloppy.

Emily heard the clarity of a fly
at the moment her life said hello
to death. Life hasn't said
a word to me, but Death is busy
speed-walking to my friend's door,
whose tired lungs are sending regrets.
All her life she's curled the hair
and put lipstick on her stories,
slanting them until they're bent.
I love them anyway, like I long to love
myself, even when I muzz the truth.

A Prayer

For the men who entered my body
who no longer are able to dance,
for nights so full of darkness I
invent a story about the sun,
for butterflies and birds that no longer
mimic a rainbow,

for big snows in Michigan
that cover sound, but forget
to show up, for a moon reaching through
a web of fog for the sake of lovers
but when I hold out my hand,
nothing is there,

for those who've always done
whatever they were told, for myself
when a mood drained of hope
makes me read sonnets all day,
and for a dead bluebird on the patio
that sings only to a gang of ants.

The Migraineur Whose Brain Misfires

Why do I try to think when a hundred teeth
are biting inside me,

why is it I insist on entering mirrors when
blank faces that live there refuse to look back,

why when I listen to the moon and hear
her story, she refuses to hear mine,

why do I keep company with bees though
they never invite me into their house,

why do I listen to the dark when its knife edge
holds up my sleep,

why is it when spring breezes blow
on my dreams, night lets dawn crack

open their shape and sound, leaving me
empty?

Job Description

What are your qualifications?

Playing Old Maid with a girl dying of leukemia.
My cane's so magical it dances after taking a nap.

What schools have you attended?

A boy named Jack.
My white hair.

Briefly describe your best and worst characteristics.

I find words riding down the air like dust motes.
When sadness thickens a day, I cry if it can't lift its head.

Who are your references?

Silk scarves that fight for dominance.
Children who can't escape the needle but try.

What are your hobbies?

I always count butterflies to see if the world is broken.
I look for the boy who can tell the moon to open her eyes.

What is your most important goal?

I want to wear the smell of mulberries stuck
between my fingers and the wind when I leave.

About the Author

Mary Carolyn Muehlmann Sesso grew up in Frankfort, Michigan. She attended the Mercy School of Nursing in Ann Arbor, holds a BA from the University of Maryland, and after retiring from her nursing career, received an MFA from Vermont College. She's lived in Maryland most of her life where she raised her family and worked at NIH and the National Children's Center. She now volunteers at NCC and sits on the Human Rights Committee.

A member of the Writer's Center in Bethesda, Maryland and three writing groups, she has written two chapbooks, *The Open Window* (Finishing Line Press, 2018, a finalist in the 2019 Comstock Review chapbook contest) and *Her Hair Plays with Fire* (Finishing Line Press, 2022). Sesso's poem "Dinner Companion" was nominated for a Pushcart Prize. Her latest work is published in *Loch Raven Review, Medical Literary Messenger, One Art, Emerge Literary Review, Ravens Perch,* and *Mid Atlantic Review.*

www.ingramcontent.com/pod-product-compliance
Lightning Source LLC
Chambersburg PA
CBHW071113090426
42737CB00013B/2589